The Joy of Hats

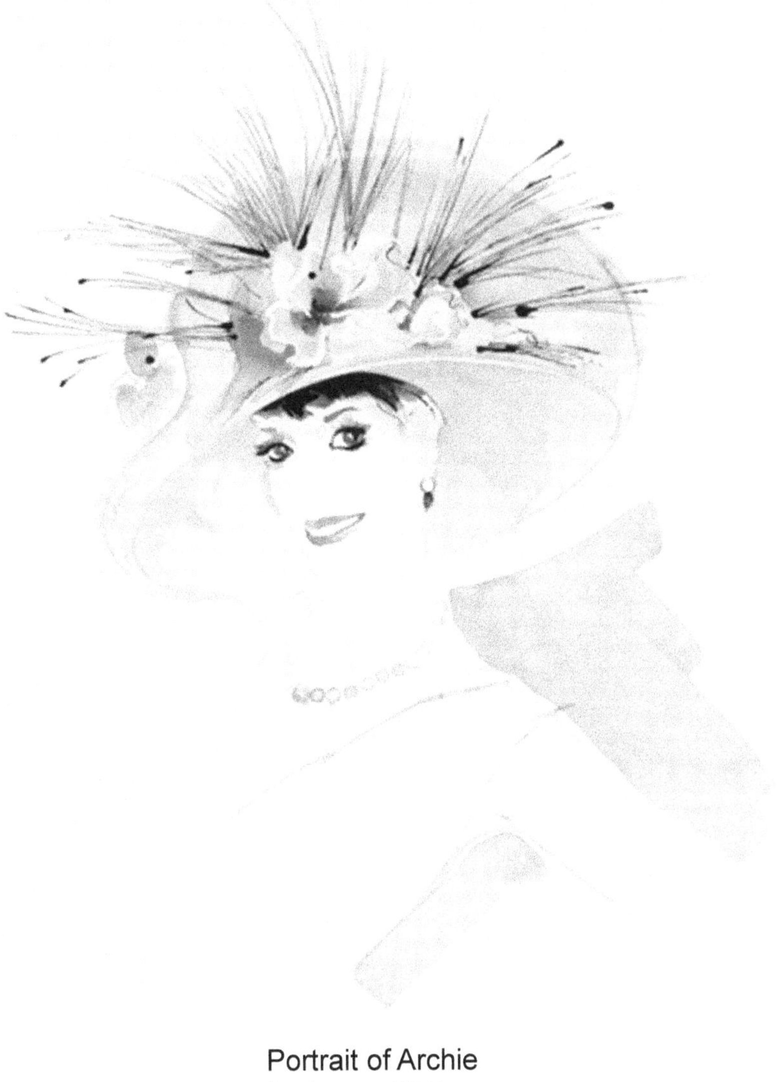

Portrait of Archie
by Lynne Riding
www.lynneriding-art.com

Presenting Everything You Ever Wanted To Know About Hats

&

Are Ready To Ask

Nat King Cole sang, "Unforgettable. That's what you are." The same can be said about hats. Moreover, when it comes to hats, add the words "timely" and "timeless," because that's what they are, too.

You are seeing headlines from the *L.A. Times*, *Vanity Fair*, and *Charleston Magazine* declaring "Hats are Back on Top" and calling them "Fall's Most Coveted Accessory" and "statement-makers." You are noticing them on the heads of men, women, and children. But hats have always been there, and hats will always be here: They belong to every culture and religion; they identify countless professions; they provide protection from the elements; they make a fashion statement. And they are something more, as you are about to find out.

Whether you are a hat lover who can't resist shopping for a new one or the hat wannabe who is afraid to toss your hat in the ring or someone who has wanted to hang up your hat, *The Joy of Hats* proves:

- There is a hat for every head that wants one
- There is a right way to shop, then care, for hats
- There is more to hat wearing than meets the eye

The Joy of Hats is a comprehensive guide with practical tips and inspirational messages. All it takes is a hat on your head and a smile on your face, and your world becomes a better place. In fact, the whole world becomes a better place. Try one on for size and discover there is a reason hats and magic go together.

Hatfully,

Archie

Table of Contents or Hat-a-Gories

Uncovering The Joy in Hats

Someone said, "If you have something important to say, say it in the beginning. My Sophomore English teacher said we "...should be able to summarize a 20 page term paper in one sentence." It will only take me ONE word to say what is most important about hats:

FUN

It is **fun** to put one on, take one last look in the mirror, and see what a hat has added to your overall appearance. You will smile at yourself.

It is **fun** to walk down the street, sit at a stoplight, or enter a room and be complimented. People will smile at you.

It is **fun** to have doors opened for you, literally and figuratively, because you put a hat on your head. You will keep smiling.

It is **fun** to learn hat wearing doesn't take confidence; it gives you confidence. (Phillip Treacy) You will always be smiling.

Magicians use hats for their tricks because the hat itself is magical:

Hats can turn plain into pizzazz, crank up the volume until the whole world sings along, change a girl into a woman and a woman back into a girl.*

Hats are shameless flatterers, calling attention to an escaping curl, a tawny braid, a sprinkling of freckles over a pert nose, directing the eye to what is most unique about a face. Their curves emphasize a shining pair of eyes, a lofty forehead; its deep brim accentuates the pale tint of a cheek, creates an aura of prettiness, suggests a mystery that awakens curiosity in the onlooker (Jeanine Larmothe).

Hats are a flag, a shield, a bit of armor, and a badge of femininity. They are the difference between wearing clothes and wearing a costume; the difference between being dressed and being dressed up; the difference between looking adequate and looking your best. Hats are to be stylish in, glow under, flirt beneath, make all others seem jealous over, and make all men feel masculine about. A piece of magic is a hat (Martha Sliter, Author).

Women** wearing hats are at once sophisticated and whimsical.... Their faces are younger and softer. They carry themselves differently, daintily, like deer. Their voices flutter a bit...even when they are talking about things like money and power and work, even when it's clear they're very much in charge of their lives ("O" Magazine).

Women are transformed when they put on a hat: Self-confidence and self-respect show in their face. They accept their femininity; they stand tall with shoulders back, even when their derriere is clothed in jeans or slacks. When my Mother first dressed me in a hat as if I were a Lady, I owned the title (*Crowns*).

(Few) women have ever been able to resist the temptation to try on a hat and discover in the mirror a person they never suspected was there. A hat alters the image we have of ourselves and the image others see as well. For the hours we wear it, it brings out a different dimension in our personality, much as a costume aids an actress in her role.

*There will be a number of quotes throughout *The Joy of Hats*. I do not always know who should be credited; I began collecting these gems long before I decided to write it.

**Although this Book addresses girls and women, men and boys also understand the joy of hats. They know they love them on themselves. They know they look good in them. They know the fun they pull from them. Thanks to *The Joy of Hats*, they will know what to do with them!

Proving You Can Look Good in a Hat

I can hear some of you saying, "I like hats. But I don't look good in them." "Saying you don't look good in hats is like saying you don't look good in shoes." (Kelly Boler) While every hat is not for every man or woman, there **is** a hat for every man or woman who wants to wear one. All you have to do is understand which one is right for you.

You will understand...at the drop of a hat...if you trust the rules found in this crash course: **Hat Wearing 101**. More detailed explanations of each point will be found throughout *The Joy of Hats*.

Introduction: The Anatomy of a Hat

There are two main parts to a hat: The crown sits atop the head. It is the upper part of the hat that gives it its height. The crown rests on the brim, which serves as a rim or border, giving the hat its width.

Rule #1: Choose a hat where the shape of the crown is different from the shape of your face. Take a good look in the mirror at your jaw line. Is it round? Square? Heart-shaped? Oval? There is nothing good or bad about the shape of your jaw line. It is what it is.

Once you have decided what that shape is, take a good look at the design of the crown of the hat. What shape is **it**? If it is the same shape as your jaw line, it is the wrong shape for your face. If its outline is different from your jaw line, you will like what you see.

Here is a great example: I love this hat. I love it so much I bought it, even though it is the same shape as my jaw line. Cute as it may be, this hat is not flattering to me:

See what happens when I put on a round crown...

...then a square crown. They both work well

Even better, see what happens when I put on an asymmetrical crown.

This crown is universally flattering because faces are generally balanced.

Rule #2: Recognize your hair is already covering your head.
Some hairstyles work better than others with having a hat added on top of them. The toughest length is one that covers the ears and extends midway between the ears and the shoulder.

I am fortunate. My hair is already out of the way.

See what happens when I put on a wig, then a hat. Even with a crown that is flattering to my jaw line, the effect is unflattering. It looks as if I am wearing two hats.

Do not despair. There is a simple solution: Get your hair out of there. Put it behind your ears or into the hat itself. Decide that that day you are choosing to wear your hat, not your hair.

Even short hair like mine may need some tweaking. My hat looks best if I tuck my bangs away:

With your hair out of the picture, you will be as pretty as a picture.

Rule #3: Position your hat on your head properly.

You are not Rebecca of Sunnybrook Farm.

Nor should your hat just sit there.

Bring that hat forward.

Cock it to the side. Tilt it mysteriously over one eye.

You are ready to toss your hat in the fashion ring and experience the joy the right hat and hatitude bring. From now on, it's Hats On!

Analyzing Your Facial Characteristics

You are ready to toss your hat in the ring, but you have to find one first. Before you look in the store, you must look in the mirror at home. You learned in Hat Wearing 101 that the crown of a hat should be any shape <u>except</u> the shape of your jaw line.

Understanding what that shape is will help you choose the most flattering crown shape. In reality, you are applying the same logic you use when buying any article of clothing. We all have styles that work best for our body shape; now we're focusing on our face.

Remember: The **Crown** is the part of the hat that is in direct contact with your head and gives you height; the **brim** is the outer rim that frames your face and gives you width.

Round: If your jaw line is round and you put on a hat with a rounded crown or down-turned brim, it exaggerates the fullness to your face. Slim it with broad brims and wide, square-shaped crowns. The crown should not be narrower than your face unless it is extended by trim. Set the brim at an angle to add length to your face.

Square: If your jaw line is square and you put on a hat with a square crown, you are over-emphasizing the angles to your face. Soften them by selecting rounded crowns. Wide or flared brims will also work, but don't forget to tilt them forward, and to one side.

Heart-Shaped: If your jaw line comes to a point, avoid pointy crowns or sharp angles. Emphasize your eyes by finding hats with short, uneven brims and lofty crowns.

Oval: If your jaw line is oval and you put on a hat with an oval crown, it tends to flatten your features. Round and square crowns work best. Go for full brims and trim that lift the eye.

The crown that is flattering to everyone? One that is **Asymmetrical**, i.e. where one side of the crown is higher than the other. After all, it is rare that someone has an angled jaw line.

There is no good or bad shape to one's face; it is what it is. Like every other part of our body, there are styles that are more flattering than others. As Milliner Vonda Parker says, "There is a hat for every woman, no matter how her face is shaped."

Considering Other Physical Characteristics

There are a few more physical characteristics to consider in selecting hats that are right for you.

Prominent Facial Features

Wearing a hat can be the perfect means to draw attention away from facial features that aren't as attractive as you would like them to be. Your hat becomes the focal point, especially hats with a forward movement and peak.

Height of Lady

If you are a short lady, start with smaller brims but do not stop there. As your confidence grows, so can the size of your hat. But select ones of lighter materials; otherwise, they will overpower you. Whichever size you choose, go for taller crowns and upturned brims to give you the illusion of height.

If you are a tall lady, you will look better with flatter crowns and wider brims. Stand up straight, even though your hat is obviously making you taller. You can minimize the size of a large hat by carrying it well.

In either case, the height of a hat should be proportionate to your body; its width should not be wider than your shoulders. This point is particularly important for the short lady, lest she end up looking out of proportion.

Complexion

Because a hat is worn so close to your face, it is important the color of the hat flatters your skin tone. If you have pale skin, a warm color such as pink or rust is a good choice. Darker skin tones are easier to match. However, if the shade is very dark, it is best to avoid black.

The Golden Rule, which trumps all the rules: Wear a hat in which you feel comfortable and confident. It should fit both you and the occasion. If you believe you look good, then you probably do! An important corollary: Don't let anyone talk you into buying a particular hat. Go with your instincts; you will never wear it!

Now let's go shopping!

Since 1868, The Bollman Hat Company has continuously produced hats for the finest brands carried in stores throughout the world: Bailey, Bailey Western, Country Gentlemen, Eddy Bros., Helen Kaminski, Ignite, Pantropic, Plaza Suite, Private Label, Relentless by Bailey. In stores throughout the U.S.

www.bollmanhats.com

Hats in the Belfry

Hats in the Belfry is an online store for men and women's hats, carrying the largest selection of hats at affordable prices.

www.hatsinthebelfry.com

The 104-year-old HeadwarAssociation is the oldest trade association in the fashion industry. Its mission is to promote hats and hardware throughout the world and to foster goodwill and fellowship among those in the industry.

www.theheadwearassociation.org.

Shopping for Hats

Phone a friend and take him or her with you! If you have a dress to match, take that with you, too.

Try on different styles

When it comes to types of women's hats, there aren't as many different styles as there are for men. In fact, small, medium, and large almost cover them. Be that as it may, there are some specific ones:

Caps: Not the baseball variety. They are feminine takes on the traditional engineer and jockey cap; the newsboy and pub caps. Wear them when you want to be casual, yet stylish. They imply, "I am doing more than covering your head."

Fedora: Yes! The classic male fedora has found acceptance on the female head with or without modification. According to Don Rongione, President and CEO of Bollman Hats, there is even a feminine fedora - summer floppy hybrid. The feminine fedora elevates the cute cap while retaining the casual look needed for mundane activities. It is a stylish unisex hat that can still look very sexy. Best of all, a fedora works day or night. Adding a flower or feather is purely optional.

Cloche: The vision that most closely defines the cloche is that of the hat worn by flappers in the Roaring 20's. Despite its vintage roots, it has never gone out of style. It works well at night when the tendency is to downsize.

Luncheon hats/Church hats: These hats shout elegance. They are a cut above the rest in size and detail.

Lampshades/Noticeables: I call the grandest hats "lampshades" because that is how they look to me. Phillip Treacy calls them "noticeables." They are worn for the most special and visible occasions of them all, such as Easter or a hat contest; they are the true statement hat.

Cocktail hats: Traditionally the smallest hats, worn for a night out. If they have a veil, all the better; it is a wonderful accessory for flirting. They work well when going to the theater because typically they are not blocking the view of people sitting around you.

Fascinators (or Whimsies): The latest trend in hats, falling in size somewhere between the small cocktail hat and medium size full hat. Since they go with cocktail dresses as well as with slacks, fascinators can be worn day or night. They attach to a head band or comb, sit atop the head, and frequently feature a creative design.

As for your collection, you might want to follow Ms. Piggy's advice: "It is vital to have at least one hat for each of the ten types of social occasions: Very formal, not so formal, just a teensy bit formal, informal, but not that informal. Every day, every other day. Day travel, night travel. Theater and fling."

In all seriousness, if you embrace the joy of hat wearing, you will eventually have some of each style, each color, appropriate for each season.

Try on a broad assortment of designs and colors. Do as Amy Smith of Portobello Hats says, "Give yourself permission to play." Find your comfort zone. Let the fun begin in what you will come to consider the ultimate candy store: The Hat Department.

Try on brims and crowns with different widths and heights. The more you experiment, the more you learn which are most flattering to you.

Try on hats in front of a three way mirror. If the store doesn't have one, ask for a hand held mirror to use in conjunction with whatever they do have. In a pinch, use a compact mirror. You must view the hat from all four sides to make a good decision. Finally place the hat on your friend's head. Ask her to walk around so you can see it in action.

As you shop, keep asking yourself:
Why am I buying this hat (motivation)?
When will I wear it (time of day/year)?
What do I want to do with it (purpose)?
Where will I wear it (occasion)?

A final word of shopping advice: Do not pass up a hat that looks great just because you don't have a dress to go with it. If anything, it is easier to find the right dress than the right hat. The best shopping guide for hats or anything else is, "I shoulda bought it when I saw it." If you are still thinking about an item as you walk out the store, walk right back in and buy it.

But one word of caution: Since hats are not usually returnable, make sure you know which ones already reside in your closet.

Once you are more confident in your hat shopping, check out the fabulous assortment of milliners on line and Ebay. Some have ways for you to post your photo, then place a photo of their hats on your head.

Answering Why The Hat Doesn't Look Quite Right

You have been carefully selecting the right crown according to the shape of your jaw line. But those hats still don't look quite right on you. You probably need a reminder of the second and third rules of **Hat Wearing 101**:

Rule #2: Recognize hair already covering your head

Adding a hat may make it look as if you are wearing two hats. Give the hat top billing. Compliment, do not compete, with your hair.

- "Clean" the hair from your face by getting it behind your ears. This guideline is especially important if your hair covers your ears and falls in that length between the bottom of your ear and your chin.

- Gather hair longer than chin length into a bun, ponytail, or simple knot at the nape of your neck. Even better, put all that hair up into the hat. Create a more elegant line by showing your neck.

- Conceal enough of your "fringe" hair (bangs or sideburns) so they do not overpower the hat.

A word about **Hat Hair**: Since women do not have to remove their hat all day, it should not be an issue. In fact, Philip Treacy believes, "Once a woman's hat is in place, she should not take it off during an event, even a church service. Her hair, at this point, 'looks awful--why take the hat off? It's like going somewhere and removing underwear.' "

If you anticipate removing your hat while still out, gather up your long hair with a barrette or spring clip before putting it on. When ready, release the clip; your hair still has fullness.

For shorter hair, lift it with hair spray or gel. As long as your hat wasn't too tight to begin with, curly hair will spring back to life with a few sprinkles of water.

In any case, the best reason for wearing a hat just may be it's "...for those days when your hair isn't enough." (Philip Treacy). Given the fact that 98% of us do not like our hair, we should wear hats that often.

Rule #3: Position the hat on your head properly

Find the label with the name of the designer or company inside the hat. Stand in front of the mirror and put it on with that label in back. Then start rotating the hat around your head. It should fit equally well with the label in back as it does in front; it may or may not be designed to sit comfortably on all four sides.

Next look at the trim on the hat.

- Are you a more outgoing, in your face type of gal? If so, put the flower, bow, feather, etc. front and center.

- Do you prefer being coy or demur? If so, place the decoration in back. Walk on by, knowing the surprise you're giving your admirers.

- Is your personality somewhere in between? If so, the decoration might be on the side of your hat, so admirers can catch you coming and going.

With the direction of your hat determined, focus on its placement:

- Few hats are designed to sit straight on or far back on your head

- A hat tilted mysteriously over one eye and/or forward at a seemingly precarious angle adds pizzazz to the plainest hat.

Hat placement cannot be overemphasized. Hats on the back of the head should be reserved for little girls. Forget *Rebecca of Sunnybrook Farm*; think Ingrid Bergman of *Casablanca*. "The great hat principle is that when you meet a woman on the street and her hat allows you to see whether she's a brunette, a blond, or a redhead, the woman in question is not wearing a chic hat...." ('The Saleswoman' in *Collected Stories*).

Let your hat take control. Whether small, fanciful, aristocratic, simple or ostentatious, the hat is everything. Give it a chance. Work it...and your hatitude along with it.

Achieving the Best Fit

Every woman knows her shoe size; few know her hat size. Unfortunately, it wouldn't matter if they did; hats that are mass produced and found in the accessory section of stores do not indicate size. Men are luckier in this regard. Their finer hat shops have specific sizes on the label inside the hat.

Thus everyone must go through a "trial and error" process of trying hats on and off...which is far more fun than tedious.

Do not be discouraged if the hat you try on does not immediately fit. There are a number of tricks that can be pulled out of that hat to make it work and help you decide whether or not to buy it.

Start by leaving the hat on for 5 minutes.

- If you feel pressure, it is too small
- If it slips or shifts when you turn your head from side to side, it is too big
- If you can slide an index finger between your head and the hat, it fits correctly
- "If you can run and go about your daily business without touching, holding onto your hat, or adjusting it all the time, then you've got a good hat" (Waltraud Reiner)

Hat Tricks you can try at the store

- If the hat is too large: If it is not way too large, you may still be able to make it work. There is a simple way to find out: Stuff the crown with a plastic bag, bubble wrap, or tissue paper from behind the counter or paper towels from the rest room. Chances are excellent they will do the trick, and the hat will fit.

- If the hat is too small: Put it back. You should not buy a hat that is too small any more than you should buy a pair of shoes that are too tight; neither the shoes nor the hat will give. You will wind up with sore feet from the former and a headache from the latter.

Hat Tricks that will work anywhere

After you purchased the hat you thought fit properly, it is possible you will start losing it with the slightest breeze or pushing it up off your forehead as your hair flattens and gravity takes its toll.

- Use safety pins (one or two will do) on the inside ribbon of the crown to tighten the fit. That's where the expression "pinhead" came from!

- Buy decorative hat pins, most often found at antique stores. If your hair is thin and can't be styled into a knot, roll a knee high stocking into a ball and attach it to your head with bobby pins. It will serve as a "pin cushion" for the hat pin.

- Purchase weather stripping or Dr. Scholl's pads and place it at the base of the crown

- Fold a big plastic bag and place it inside your hat. Not only will it take up extra space, it will protect your hat from a sudden downpour. Better to get your hair wet than your hat!

- Find Super Sliders, (carried at most general stores). They are felt pads with an adhesive backing that fit under furniture to keep it from sliding or scratching the surface on which it sits. Place as many as needed at the base of the crown to achieve a secure fit. Buy strips, not dots.

Do Not ever use double sided tape to hold the hat to your head. It will pull your hair out when you take your hat off!

Do reach for a plastic bag, bubble wrap, or paper hand towels from the restroom for those emergencies when your hat starts slipping and annoying you, and you are far from home. Just stuff 'em in there, and enjoy the rest of the day.

Custom Designed Hats or Those Purchased from Milliners

When working directly with a milliner, your hat will be made to order. Therefore, you will need to <u>know your hat size</u>:

Measure around your head where a hat would sit (normally about 1/2"-1" above the eyebrows and ears). Hold the tape measure comfortably, as you would like a hat to fit (most measuring errors occur by applying the tape too tightly). If you do not have a flexible tape measure, a piece of string or ribbon (non stretchy) can be held around the head, then measured on a yardstick.

If your measurement puts you exactly between two sizes, it is generally better to select the larger of the two. It is better to adjust the fit of a slightly loose hat than to think you can stretch one that is too tight.

A Bit More About Fit

The extremes in head size can be accommodated

<u>Ladies with small heads</u>

- Find a store catering to those who have undergone chemotherapy (often a hospital gift shop). They are particularly sensitive to the need for hats with small crowns. An extra bonus: These hats often have big brims that provide sun protection.

- Look for hats with adjustable bands or drawstrings built into the crown

- Check out stores for pre-teens and buy fedoras and caps

- Explore vintage clothing and antique stores; heads tended to be smaller in those days

- Search the internet for milliners who accommodate the smaller head or make customized hats

Ladies with large heads

- Inspect the inside of the hat to determine if the inner hat band can be carefully slit or cut out entirely to add precious space

- Look for hats with adjustable bands or drawstrings built into the crown

- Search the internet for milliners who accommodate the larger head or make customized hats

Ladies who have suffered hair loss due to medical conditions

- Find stylish hats that turn a "need" to wear them into a "want" to wear them

- Log onto a special web site designed for you: www. headcovers.com (along with other millinery web sites)

The hat must fit your personality

- Choose another style if you have doubts about it. Just like the shoe analogy, you will not grow into comfortably wearing it. Never buy a hat only because it looks good on the rack.

- Whether your head is small or big, there's a hat for you, somewhere a hat for you. Of course, when you find it, never let it go. Save the name of the designer and buy more!

Pulling it all Together

As important as it is to find the right hat, it should never be viewed as a separate item from the rest of your outfit. What makes or breaks your look is coordinating yourself from top to bottom.

You may actually shop less if you start adding hats to items already hanging in your closet. It is called "shopping your closet." It is a perfect way to keep your clothes from becoming old hat. But if you cannot resist the temptation to shop, here are some guidelines:

Clothing: It is best to choose a simple outfit if you are wearing an especially noticeable hat. "If you are wearing a statement hat, then I wouldn't wear a statement dress." (Phillip Treacy) Even the simplest of hats dresses up the plainest of clothes -- from jeans to dresses to beachwear. A hat makes you look snappy!

Then Accessorize, Accessorize, Accessorize

www.Hatlife.com tells us accessories are getting increased space in the stores and in the curriculum of fashion institutes; they have become just as important as clothes.

Jewelry: The key to adding to, not detracting from, your hat statement is to keep proportion in mind when selecting jewelry. A hat and hair (to some extent) already surround your face. Select small earrings unless you are wearing a very large brimmed hat. In that case, bigger than usual earrings will provide balance. Otherwise, they are too much.

The "too much" rule also applies to necklaces or pins. You do not want to crowd all this interest swirling around your face to the point where nothing stands out. If anything is worn tight to the neck, let it be something delicate. A chunky necklace or pin is acceptable as long as it hangs down a distance from the hat.

Glasses: Wearing a hat can be the perfect way to draw attention away from them. But there are some hat styles that work better with glasses than others:

- Select hats with turned up brims. Those wearing heavier and darker colored frames should avoid larger and down-turned brims

- Choose brims that swoop up on one side as well as asymmetrical shapes

- Avoid hats that just sit there

Shoes and Purses: Ladies who love hats tend to love shoes. So have fun shopping for some killer shoes to match, (but don't let them kill your feet)!

Knowing Where And When To Wear Hats

WHERE:

According to Le Fleur Millinery in New Orleans, "Wear your hats at places of worship and worship services; art galleries and museums; brunch, lunch, tea or dinner; opera, symphony or theater; weddings, bar and bat mitzvahs, christenings and confirmations; horse races; beach, park, or botanical garden; black tie gala; parties and receptions; shopping; and...

...anywhere else you wish and for as long as you wish."

Actually the only place you do not wear a hat is at a function in your own house. In that case, wearing a hat suggests you have some place better to go.

"By the way, you must always wear a hat when lunching with people you do not know well. It is to your advantage to appear to your best advantage." (source unknown)

WHEN:

Time of day
I really did not want to include this section and place limitations on hat wearing now that you are finally wearing them. My personal guideline is if it matches what you are wearing, then wear it, regardless of its size and shape, regardless of the time of day.

But there are purists out there. So here are two guidelines from Miss Manners that appeared in the brochure from Le Fleur Millinery

- If the hat looks as if you had it built, it may properly go to daytime functions. Brims should be reserved for daytime wear.

- If the hat looks as if it has just landed in your hair (bits of feather, sequins, or whatever), it goes out at night.

Time of Year

There are also traditionalists in regards to wearing certain materials. In this case, my personal guideline is based more on color (pastels in spring; white and light in the summer; gold, brown, red, orange, dark green in autumn; black, gray, silver in winter).

Moreover, the climate where you live should be a major factor in determining how heavy a material you wear throughout the year. However, I would avoid a light straw hat in the winter, no matter how warm the temperature.

Additional guidelines from Le Fleur:

Spring and Summer: Straw, lace, taffeta, tulle, linen, satin, lightweight fabrics.

Fall and Winter: Felt or velour, leather and suede, velvet, wool, corduroy, heavier fabrics.

Year-round evening hats: Silk, chiffon, crepe, lace, organza, taffeta, tulle, satin, jersey, brocade, beaded fabric, embroidered fabric.

Conquering Hat Anxiety

You have found it! Now it is time to wear it. When you do, men will desire. Women will envy. You'll wonder why the heck you never did it before.

First, however, you may need to conquer **Hat Anxiety**. I believe this term was coined by Kelly Boler in 'Put a Lid on It,' *A Few Heady Thoughts on Women's Hats*. Whatever the source, this section is a combination of their words and my own.

Hat anxiety is the impulse that overwhelms you when you're about to leave your house with a hat carefully placed on your head. As you approach your party or wedding (the typical events where you will even dare to wear one), you become increasingly uneasy. You are certain people are looking at you. In this vulnerable moment, you panic, suffer an attack of hat anxiety, and leave your hat in the car.

Here are some tips on overcoming this fear of commitment to hat wearing:

- Trick yourself into wearing hats. Cold dreary winter weather and hot sunny summer weather give you an excuse to try something more daring without feeling outrageous

- Wear hats while on vacation or at places you have never been before. Those seeing you won't realize you don't wear them all the time. Others will get used to seeing you in hats, and you will, too. Then it will be easier for you to wear them around people you already know. As a bonus, you will become accustomed to having people talk to you and complimenting you (though it never becomes old hat....)

- Wear a simple hat, such as a beret, so you are comfortable keeping it on when you arrive at your destination

- Wear a hat with something plain or classic, like a black dress or gray suit. An understated look, paired with a hat, will help you avoid feeling you are wearing a costume and making an entrance

- Wear men's hats. Fedoras, boaters, and derbies look great with women's clothing. Just add a pin or silk flowers to soften the look and coordinate the rest of your look

- Jump. Just do it. Find a hat that makes you happy and stop thinking about it. Admirable as she was, do not be like Erma Bombeck, in this regard:

"I have a hat. It is graceful and feminine and has a wide brim with a red ribbon around the band. It gives me a certain dignity, as if I were attending a state funeral or something. People are generous in their compliments. Someday I may get up enough courage to wear it, instead of carrying it." (from Women Who Wear Hats Stand Heads Above the Rest).

Do not wait too long to muster your courage. Put a smile on your face, a hat on your head, and "**walk into a room as if you own the place**" (Skirt! Magazine)

This tip is the best of all, regardless of what's on your head.

However, if you happen to be wearing a hat, you will be admired by writers like Kelly Boler, who describes her struggle with Hat Anxiety:

"I know I am generalizing, but I'm bitter. In my heart, I know there is much to admire about a woman wearing a hat who knows that she attracts the attention of every eye around her and can still walk like a person. I used to give speeches, and I'd be so self-conscious I'd walk to the podium as though I were marching into Poland.

Throughout the years, I have mentally put together a profile of women who can wear hats. Generally, they are women of great confidence. When they visit someone in the hospital, they park their car in the tow away zone. It is always there when they return for it. Their hair is always long enough on the sides to pull back and secure without little pieces standing out over their ears like Howdy Doody.

They love blueberries, and they never stain their teeth. They have two children: A boy and a girl, who are not allowed to watch television. Their husbands recite them poetry that doesn't rhyme. They're the first to wear white shoes in the spring. The family dog wears braces for an overbite.

Every Easter Sunday the hat wearers will be out in force: Those who are comfortable in them, and those who would not feel more conspicuous if two wombats were mating on their head."

Once you overcome Hat Anxiety, you will never go back to being bareheaded again. Your friends will feel your confidence, and they will start wearing them, too....particularly when they notice the favorable reaction you are getting from the opposite sex.

Go Ahead and Bloom (a Philosophy)

"It is time to drop our camouflage and take power as women," said Anais Nin. "There comes a time when the risk to remain tight in the bud is more painful than the risk it takes to blossom.

When you wear a hat, it is like medicine for the soul. The hat is the expression of who we are as women in every moment! The hat is our dreams of who you can be. It facilitates the different parts of who you are. With the wave of the hat, Viola! You are mysterious...no, you are sexy; now proper; now playful.

You cannot hide in a hat. You will be noticed--especially by men. To men you become a lady when you don a hat--one which they rush to open doors for. To women you become an inspiration, reminding them that they have a closet full of hats they have not had the courage to wear."

Following Hat Etiquette (Hatiquette)

1. Don't touch someone's hat

2. Don't get too close to someone's hat when admiring it, lest you knock it off

3. Don't get too close when hugging someone wearing a hat. Tilt your head to the side. If two hat wearers hug, both must tilt her head to the side in opposite directions and leave space in between. Blow a kiss or shake hands instead

4. Don't get too close if you are wearing a hat and having a picture taken with someone also wearing one. It is better to leave a space in between than to capture your head at an odd angle

5. Don't block the view of others in church, theater, or stadiums. Ask those around you if your hat interferes. If so, take it off when the lights go out. Avoid this problem altogether and select seats off to the side or in the back rows

6. Don't ask to borrow someone's hat. Some Ladies would lend their children before they'd lend their hats. They know their children can find their way home, but their hats might not.

7. Don't get jealous. Women who love hats are happy to see a hat that looks good on someone else. Women who wear hats know who they are. They have just the right hatitude.

 * I do not know where the term "Hatiquette" comes from. I might have been inspired to coin it myself after reading *Crowns*, a classic that tells the stories of Black women and their church hats. In any case, the essence of most of these guidelines is taken from that Book.

Handling, Storing, Decorating, Cleaning, Repairing, Traveling

You have been shopping, fitting, coordinating, and best of all, wearing! What are the other 'ing's you need to know?

Handling

- Never pick up a hat unless your hands are clean. Lift it by placing one hand on the back of the brim and the other on the front

- Never pick up a hat by the crown. Doing so crushes the crown and can cause it to become misshapen.

- Never wear your hat unprotected in inclement weather -- particularly straws and sinamay (sinamay is a loose weave, often see-thru)

- Remember to place a large plastic bag inside the crown to pull out, in case of rain

Storing

There is one overriding guideline for storing your hats: **Do not rest them on their brim:**

Use the following items instead:

<u>Hat Stand</u>

Ideally use a stand designed for this purpose, especially for hats with floppy brims or elaborate trim. These stands allow the hat to hang as it would on your head and its trim rest undisturbed.

- However, common household items can substitute, provided steps are taken to cushion the crown: A roll of paper towels, balanced on one end

- A wine bottle

- Candle sticks

- Coffee cans stacked on top of one another

Either stuff a ball of <u>acid free tissue paper</u> into the crown or cut a Styrofoam ball in half and place it on the spot where the hat will rest on the above items. You need to prevent anything pointy from damaging the crown.

<u>Shelves and Hat Boxes</u>: Your goal remains keeping hats off their brims

- If you have one hat on the shelf or in the box, turn it crown side down and stuff the crown with acid free paper to hold its shape

- If you have more than one hat on the shelf or in the box, turn them all crown side down and "nest" the crown of one hat into the crown of another. In this case, the crown itself takes the place of the acid free tissue paper. This type of stacking maximizes the number of hats filling the space

- Purchase large, clear (transparent) containers with PC that block out moisture

- Take photos of the hat(s) inside each box and paste them on the outside. Use an index card to describe the clothes worn with them and paste it next to the photo

- Store them in clear plastic dry cleaning bags, then lay them on shelves arranged by color

- Store them under a bed in a guest room, brims upside down, of course

Decorating

Since closet space is always at a premium, bring out those hats! Some of the ideas just mentioned lend themselves to wonderful decorative touches throughout your house:

- Choose lamps that do not provide critical light and replace their shade with a hat that complements its surroundings. **Remove the light bulb first**, lest you or a guest inadvertently turn on the lamp

- Purchase hat boxes with attractive prints and colors that match your decor. Place (and stack) them in corners of your rooms. They can even be used as small tables

- Find attractive hooks, then hang your hats on the wall of a room or the wall going up to your second floor

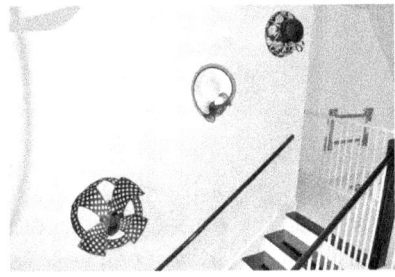

- Create your own hat rack by purchasing a rectangular piece of plywood at least 6" wide and 3' long (depending on how many hats will be displayed). Paint the plywood, then attach decorate door knobs. That's giving you something to hang your hat on

- Decorate a Christmas tree with hats, purses, and pearls

- Make a centerpiece for a table using hats and flowers

- Purchase an attractive breakfront, place it in a prominent spot, and fill its shelves with your favorite hats

- Keep all hats in dry, cool places away from direct sunlight and dust them regularly

Naturally the hats themselves can be decorated. Not only will it be less expensive to purchase a plain hat, then add flowers, feathers, pins, ribbons, etc., the result will be one of a kind. Then too, you can redecorate them before they become "old hat." Supplies can be found on line or at craft stores.

Cleaning

Invest in two good brim brushes--one with dark bristles for dark colored hats and one with light colored bristles for light colored hats. Brush hats regularly in a clockwise direction to keep dust from settling into the fibers. Light colored hats should be brushed more often. Clean your brushes after each use to avoid transferring fibers of one hat to a hat of another color.

All substances recommended below should be tested on a part of the hat that is not outwardly visible (i.e. inside the crown) to determine if they will aggravate the condition rather than improve it

Straw Hats

- To clean an organic stain, try peroxide; otherwise use a dry cleaning solvent. Apply one or the other, then blot it from both sides until it is almost dry. Repeat the process after it dries, if needed. Do not use bleach since it will yellow the straw

- To restore luster, rub gently with very fine sandpaper. Brush regularly with a soft brim brush, whisk broom, or damp cloth

- To remove dirty marks, gently wipe with a damp cloth. If unsuccessful, use a small amount of dry cleaning fluid on a cotton ball

- To completely rejuvenate, spray paint it, using the paint for silk flowers found at a crafts store; it will not break down the fibers

Felt Hats. All these products and methods have merit:

- Very fine sandpaper (or soft brush), rubbed softly

- Gonzo for picking up pet hair

- Dry cleaning fluid (e.g. "Renuzit" and "Energine") on a soft cloth with a short nap

- Art gum eraser rubbed in a counter clock-wise motion to the grain of the brim

- Fuller's Earth for oily stains; use plastic or rubber sponge to apply

- Scout Hat Cleaner purchased from a milliner

- Dryel Stain Remover

- Professional hat cleaner and/or milliner; NOT a clothes cleaning establishment

To keep decorations on your hats clean and fresh: Steam the hat over a pot of boiling water for a few seconds until trim softens. Smooth and hold in position until cool.

To prevent hats from wilting and protect from raindrops: Buy inexpensive hats, then spray them with clear acrylic on both sides. Use flat finish.

Repairing

Take good care of them in the first place! Keep them out of direct sunlight and protect from being squashed or crumpled. But don't hang up your hat if they are damaged. Invest in a Styrofoam head on which to place the hat once you have tried these procedures:

For a hat with dents: Boil water in a pot. Once it is steaming freely, turn down the heat. But keep steam coming out gently. Use pot holders that cover your hands.

Position the affected area over the steam and allow the steam to penetrate the straw or felt. Keep moving the hat around in order for the heat to spread evenly in and around the material. Work in small sections, removing hat from steam after 20-30 seconds.

Quickly push out the dent or rework the shape with your fingers. Blow on the repaired patch to cool it. The material will stiffen. It is also possible to stiffen the hat by steaming the felt or straw thoroughly and allowing it to cool. The stiffener will soften when hot but re-bonds and hardens when cooled.

Do not overdo the steaming as you can distort the hat, especially if you are working on a sharp edge or fine detail. Try not to "overwork" any area.

For a misshapen straw hat (where texture isn't too stiff or too flimsy): Stuff crown with wet towels and let it set for a few hours, crown down. Then flip hat over and fill crown with rolled up wet towels. Let it sit for another few hours.

A straw hat can also be ironed with a cool iron (a high setting will burn the straw). Keep moving it over the damaged area. If it's a flat brim, lay the hat on an ironing board. If the area is curved, hold a thick wad of material on one side of the straw and iron from the reverse side. For difficult repairs, use the iron to apply heat and steam, then use fingers to manipulate the straw into shape while material is still hot. (www.hatsuk.com)

For a misshapen felt hat: Do not iron felt hats; steam only. Use a Styrofoam head to prevent shrinkage in the head band area.

For velour that has gone flat: Use a stiff brush to restore nap while steaming; can be ironed.

For a brim that is wrinkled: Place a damp paper towel between brim and use an iron set on LOW heat. Press, then allow hat to dry flat. FYI: This fix may not work well on Sinamay straw. (from Kathi Harris of Hat-a-tude)

For a veil that has been crushed: Hold over steam.

For silk flowers that have been mashed: Fluff, then apply hair spray to hold the shape. Avoid getting the spray on the hat itself.

If all else fails, paint over the stains with spray paint for silk flowers or cover spots with a decorative items e.g. flower or pin.

Traveling

Don't leave home without them! Taking them along can be done at the drop of a hat.

Wear It

Wear your hat, the biggest hat you need for your trip, on the plane or train. It may be over the top, but at least you will have it with you in one piece when you arrive.

In a pinch, you can even wear two hats at the same time. This tip is particularly helpful if you find a hat while traveling and did not anticipate needing space to pack it. Just as hats nest on a shelf, they can nest on your head. How you look is not as important as having as many hats with you as possible and arriving with them in the best condition possible. Besides, hats always attract attention anyway.

Pack Inside Your Suitcase:
- Crushable hats. There is an increasing number of stylish hats for every season that are designed for this purpose. If you cannot find them in stores, google them. Many will be plain. Just buy ribbons and bows and flowers to spruce them up and coordinate with the colors of the clothing you are taking with you

- Small hats. They will fit in Tupperware containers

- Large hats. They should have the crown filled with acid free tissue paper and put in a plastic bag. Place them top side down in the middle of your suitcase. Surround the brim with acid free tissue paper or rolled up underwear and socks

Pack Others Inside a Hat Box that doubles as your Purse
- Substitute a hat box for your purse. A medium size hat box can hold 2-3 hats. It leaves room for your wallet, plane ticket, mirror, lipstick and jewelry around the perimeter of the box as well as in the crown of the hats (which of course, are upside down, off the brim and nested). The hat box should fit in an overhead bin and/or under the seat in front of you. Coordinate its colors with the colors of your traveling outfit.

- Using your hat box as your purse also allows you to have one carry-on, which may ultimately hold hats you buy on your trip

- While hard hat boxes work well for this purpose, there is a terrific soft traveling version made by Hats in The Belfry. It fits on airplanes and has more "give" because of its material.

<u>Pack in a drum case</u>

<u>Pack in a light, clear plastic bag</u> such as a dry cleaning bag, tied at one end first.

- Pack the crown tightly with acid free tissue, lay it at the bottom of the bag on open sheets of tissue and some tissue on top. It depends on the style, but usually crown down works best. If you are taking more than one hat, nest them with tissue in between.

- Tie the opposite end of the bag, capturing some air to make a bubble. Then tie it to your carry on. It will fit in the overhead or under the seat; just make sure no heavy objects are placed on top of it. Do not forget it when leaving the plane. (Kathi Harris, Hat-a-tude).

If traveling by train, all the above suggestions apply, plus you can put your hats in a big lawn bag. And if you're traveling by car, take all you want...safely, please.

Having More Fun With Hats

While wearing hats is fun, in and of itself, there are countless times one can share that joy. After all, a hat conveys to people, "I'm having a good time." (Phillip Treacy).

So have a good time:

While on the Go

You are never alone when you are wearing a hat. People of all ages and backgrounds who would have had no reason to talk to you, will talk to you. Your hat opens up communication whether you are walking down the street, filling your gas tank, sitting at a stoplight, waiting in line at the store. It may be nothing more than a honk of a horn or a thumbs up, but it always has a smile attached to it. You are even smiling at yourself and walking taller. After all, your hat would fall off, if you didn't....

Wherever you go, whatever you do, whoever you meet, you will be complimented and even photographed. You will begin to wonder how many compliments are too many and if you need a bigger hat size. Nothing increases self-esteem more than wearing a hat that elicits a response. When you look good, you feel good.

While Babysitting Children or Grandchildren

Bring your hats out of the closet. Suggest your children put together a play. It will stimulate their imagination and entertain you seeing hats used in such a happy way.

While Planning Parties

One of the simplest ways to have one of the best parties for children of all ages is to incorporate hats into the plan. Once the party gets going and people are loosened up, bring out the hats. Men and women, girls and boys will pull fun out of those hats. Have cameras handy to capture the pure joy on their faces and record the gales of laughter.

If you are making a party for little girls, make it a tea party. Buy inexpensive straw hats, flowers, ribbon, and sparkles, and begin the festivities with hat decorating. Be sure and make hats for the moms who are helping.

Sometimes people must wear hats due to illness. Throw them a Hat Party. Have everyone bring the guest of honor all types of hats to wear: Attractive, practical, sensible; wild and zany. Of course, all guests should be wearing hats, too. At the drop of a hat, you have turned something that person had to do into something he/she wants to do and had fun doing.

Incorporate a hat theme into the context of a larger party. If planning activities for a wedding where one family is coming from out of town, ask each member to decorate a hat for the rehearsal dinner that reflects his personality, travels, occupation, etc. It can be the best ice-breaker.

There is no limit to the ideas that can be pulled out of a hat when it comes to parties. While you're at it, consider making a cake or baking cookies in the form of a hat.

While Teaching
Introduce the concept of different professions through the hats that symbolize them (policeman, detective, fireman, artist, chef, etc.). Incorporate the hats worn by different cultures into geography lessons. Use storybooks about hats as part of reading lessons.

While Visiting Someone in the Hospital
If you love wearing hats, do not leave them home when visiting someone in the hospital. They will lift that person's spirits along with the spirit of staff and other patients. Remember, when you look good, you feel good. And when you feel good, it's contagious. Spread it around.

If the person you are visiting also loves hats, bring along an extra. It can be just the perk-me-up to the no make up, dreary gown, and hair style they have been wearing. In any case, they will love looking at you.

If there is a Children's Hospital nearby, gather friends and bring simple (baseball) caps for the children to decorate. My Organization, *The Hat Ladies* has been doing this Project twice a month for over eight years. Nothing lifts children's spirits more than seeing themselves in a mirror wearing a hat they designed; nothing lifts your spirit more than seeing the joy on their face.

While Visiting Assisted Living Facilities

A visit to an Assisted Living facility intended to bring cheer to a resident can bring much more if you bring along a stylish hat. What it does is stimulate their memory of pleasant times when they wore hats. In turn, it gives them something to talk about and remember days after your visit.

Even persons in the early stages of Alzheimer's Disease can benefit greatly by seeing people in hats and having one to put on. They enjoy seeing themselves in the mirror. This fact is extremely significant because those with this condition typically avoid mirrors since they don't like what they see. Administrators comment about the long-lasting positive effects of giving people something to hang their hat on.

Consider gathering a few hats and friends, contacting the Activities Director, and heading to the closest assisted living facility. You might incorporate song and dance into your visit. It will be hard to tell who has more fun...you or the residents. Just ask *The Hat Ladies*; we have also been making such visits for years.

There is no limit to the fun that can be pulled out of a hat and the joy they bring both the wearer and the observer!

Presenting Hat Facts

Books have been written about the history of hats. While they are interesting, they risk being "old hat." Here are some fun facts:

"Mad as a hatter" refers to the prevalence of brain damage workers experienced from chemicals once used in the felting process.

Mary Kies received the first U.S. patent granted to a woman in 1809. Her method of weaving straw and silk together advanced the art of hat-making.

St. Catherine is the patron saint of milliners. Young women who worked for milliners began wearing brightly colored hats in her honor; they were called catherinettes. This tradition continues today in celebrations throughout the world on November 25th.

One reason there are so few vintage hats from the late 1800's to early 1900's is they were too large to store and too difficult to clean. Drastic style changes dealt the final blow, and most were discarded.

A significant style change resulted from animal rights activists protesting the use of exotic birds as hat decorations. Feathers from domestic chickens, pheasants, or ostrich were (and remain) acceptable since they are not endangered and shed them naturally.

Hats in the 19th and 20th centuries were often so large theater managers would announce Ladies had to remove them during performances.

Hats were downsized in WWI because of shortages of material and the somber tone of the times.

After WWI, hats had to compete with the hairstyle of the day-- buns--and vice versa. Still no respectable lady went out without one.

Hat pins were a popular accessory, often worn 2-3 to a hat. Ladies would save "pin money" to buy them, hence the expression. Hat pins also served to discourage a suitor or ward off an attack. Roses were and remain the most popular flower to decorate hats.

Legend has it that President John F. Kennedy single handedly killed the hat industry by being the first President not to wear a hat to his Inauguration. While he wore a hat en route to the Ceremony, he removed it before addressing the crowd. The hat industry started to decline shortly thereafter, prompting many to believe he was the cause of its death. You can't keep a good hat down forever!

Summarizing the Principles
or
Hat-i-Chisms of Hat Wearing

The Christian doctrine has a set form of question and answer to teach its tenets, known as Catechism. *The Joy of Hats* has three questions and multiple answers; I call it Hat-i-chism:

Question: What else should you know about hats?

Answers:

Hats are like people: Sometimes they reveal; sometimes they conceal (*Crowns*).

Hats signify your "SWAG"- S-Your Sophistication, W-Your Willingness to Help Others, A-Your Attitude, and G- The Greatness in Believing in Yourself (Tammy McCottrey Brown, Talk Show Host).

Hats can bring on more shenanigans than forgetting your silk undies.

Hats make a statement, and it's not as permanent as a tattoo" (Jennifer Webley, Portobello Hats).

Hats are like punctuation marks: They make a declarative statement (a period), add mystery and intrigue (a question mark), or show a playful, fun-filled side (an exclamation point).

Hats are sculpture for the human head, which acts as a pedestal constantly moving and turning (Eia Millinery Design).

Hats are an expression of one's soul (Lilly Dache, the most famous milliner in the United States from 1924-1968).

Question: What happens to those who wear them?

Answers:

Hats take people's minds off your wrinkles.

Wearing hats is like having a baby or a puppy; everyone stops to coo and talk about them (Louise Green, Milliner); My pets are my hats. I haven't left home without a hat since the early 1980's (Anna Piaggi, Editor *Italian Vogue*).

Whenever you wear a hat, your day will be special (Margo Nickel, Milliner).

There's just something special about a woman in a hat (Betmar/ Bollman Hat Company).

Luxurious, flirty, and at times, a bit sexy; ...a great hat can change your day (Plaza Suite/Bollman Hat Company).

Wearing a hat opens up communication between people period!!! (Suzanne Flynn, Hat Lady).

We just know inside that we're queens. And these are the crowns we wear (*Crowns)*.

Women who love hats love life (Cynthia's Century of Styles).

My hat...
Is it a noun? No...
My hat is like an adjective describing me.
It bends with me and is very obedient.
It stays with me wherever I go.
My hat is more like me than anything else.
I love my hat because it is the one thing that won't annoy me.
Whether it's blue, black, pink, or tan, it stays on my head and is
very obedient
Because, after all, it is my hat
(*My Hat* by Tess Abedon)

Question: What is the best advice to be pulled out of a hat?

Answers:

With the right hat, nothing else matters.

Always leave them wondering which is the more interesting piece of work: You or your hat.

Wearing a hat versus not wearing a hat is the difference between looking adequate and looking your best.

You can flirt with a fan in your hand. You can flirt holding a cigarette, too. But a woman can really flirt with a hat (Dolores Foster, LeFleur Millinery).

Without hats we would have no civilization (Christian D'Or).

Beautify America. Wear a hat!

And the best advice of all:

Read the next chapter of *The Joy of Hats*

Understanding What Hats Can Teach Us About Life

Whether or not everyone will ever wear a hat, everyone will use expressions that contain the word "hat." Hats are an integral part of our language because they express universal truths. Thus we sometimes **pass the hat** or **keep things under our hat**.

One popular expression relates to what we do with our hats: We can hang up our hats literally; we can feel like hanging up our hats figuratively. Death of loved ones, divorce from loved ones, disappointment in things we had loved, can make the strongest among us want to **hang up our hat**. It is unlikely that any of us will go through life without occurrences that make us feel that way, to some degree. At such times, we need something **to hang our hat on**:

> "When you have come to the edge
> Of all the light that you know
> And are about to drop off into the darkness
> Of the unknown,
> Faith is knowing One of two things will happen:
>
> There will be something solid to stand on
> or
> You will be taught to fly.
>
> (Patrick Overton)

I left the life I had known for almost 50 years in Chicago for the unknown. I knew I did not want to hang up my hat. But I was not sure which new hat I would wear.

Although I had loved hats since I found them in my girlfriend's attic when we were ten years old, I began to wear them faithfully as my husband and I walked the historic streets of our new city, Charleston, South Carolina. An amazing thing began to happen: People talked to me. They complimented my hats. They shared stories of family and friends who loved hats. I began to sense I could **pull something out of a hat**.

But what? I did not want to sell them, make them, or decorate them; I only wanted to wear them. Just wearing them seemed frivolous, especially in comparison to other jobs I held and felt were meaningful. I was immobilized with uncertainty.

One day, after yet another person commented favorably on my hat, my husband gently nudged me and said, "Just take her name and email address." I did so **at the drop of a hat**. All too often we hesitate, procrastinate, bloviate, rather than act. We have to know when to follow Nike's admonition and, "Just do it."

The next thing I knew I had created *The Hat Ladies*, an Organization of Ladies of all ages who love hats of all colors. Although I felt satisfaction organizing monthly Luncheons and Hatpy Hours, I sensed more could be pulled from our hats.

I had to look outside the box, make that the hat box. I found opportunities for us to wear our hats by adding community service to camaraderie. Our motto became: "When you look good, you feel good. And when you feel good, you do good." With our mix of fashion and compassion, we became known as "...a stylish brigade of volunteers who are making a difference" (*Better Homes and Gardens*). I had found my voice and was able to inspire others to find theirs (Stephen R. Covey).

Research shows we identify our interests and exhibit our talents by the time we are ten years old. With hindsight giving me 20-20 vision, I see where what I did years ago is connected to what I am doing now. Our lives really do have a rhyme and a reason.

Be a detective in your own life. Look for those things you chose to do for hours, things your parents didn't have to remind you to do. If you can't remember what they were, ask them or your siblings or childhood friends. People often observed us engaged in activities that were so natural we took them for granted.

Moreover, they observed intangibles about us that reveal who we were and who we still are. When I told my childhood friends about *The Hat Ladies*, they responded with, "I'm not surprised." Deep down I am still that little girl in the attic finding hats, the teenage girl making luncheons for my senior class, and the young adult volunteering for good causes.

"It is never too late to be what you might have been" (George Eliot). It is never too late to rediscover and rekindle your passions. Once you have found them, examine them from every angle for their potential. Something that seems "stupid" or **old hat** may prove to be the most satisfying thing you will ever do.

When you **toss your hat in the ring** and follow your bliss, you will "...put yourself on a kind of track that has been there all the while waiting for you, and the life you ought to be living is the one you are living" (Joseph Campbell).

Therein lies a message for everyone, especially those who find themselves at a crossroad. It doesn't matter if you are in high school, in college, or in later years. The question, "What do I want to do when I grow up?" can surface. The answer has been there all along.

I am living a life different from what I thought it would be. **We all wear many hats.** It doesn't mean that one is better than the other. They are just different. Joy is still yours to pull out of whatever hat you wear, whatever life you lead. It may be joy in a different form, but it is joy, nonetheless. Keep trying different styles until you find the one that fits. Your new life may be good enough, as good, or even better than the one before. With the right hatitude, there will always be something **to hang your hat on** that brings you joy.

Taking My Hats Off To My Supporters

My hats are off to the following people who helped make *The Joy of Hats* and the joy in my life a reality:

Benjamin Goldsmith*, my paternal great grandfather, who sold hats in his dry goods store in Collinsville, Oklahoma, and to **Ted Wright**, who dug thru the archives of *The Collinsville News* to find the ads

Anna Leventhal*, my maternal grandmother, who was known as *The Hat Lady* (in Chicago) and believed in "Putting it all together"

* Coincidences I was unaware of until years after starting *The Hat Ladies*

The Hat Ladies of Charleston, who share my joy of hats and passion for making a difference in the Charleston community

Lovely **Ellen Plusker**, friend since third grade, and her Mother, beautiful **Bertha Plusker**, who never stopped believing in me and cheering me on...and up

Bernard Grossman, formerly of Betmar Hats, currently with F & M Hats, who has been my millinery muse and my trusted friend

Judy Watts, former Fashion Editor of *The Post and Courier*, now Editor of *The Summerville Journal*, whose enthusiastic columns introduced *The Hat Ladies* to the Charleston community

Diane Feen of *Hatlife* and **Becky Weaver** of Hatalk, who provided invaluable national and international publicity for *The Hat Ladies*

Dick Cote, noted author and friend, who guided me through the joys of publishing

Margaret English and **Julie Zeigler,** who shared their talents on and off the water

Naomi Shifrin Sekely, my sophomore English teacher, who helped me right so good (only kidding! Make that "write so well")

John Burkel, my husband, who is the wind beneath my wings and my everlasting joy